Holidays Around the World

Celebrate
Passover

Deborah Heiligman
Consultant, Rabbi Shira Stern

NATIONAL GEOGRAPHIC
WASHINGTON, D.C.

matzah

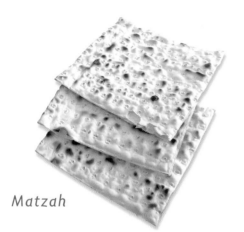

Matzah

maror

< *A family holds a seder in Yemen. The plate is filled with the symbolic foods of Passover, including three pieces of matzah.*

In spring, Jewish people all over the world celebrate Passover. We celebrate with matzah, maror, and memories.

At a special meal called the seder, we remember the story of Passover. Long ago, our ancestors, the Israelites, were slaves in Egypt. Pharaoh, the ruler of Egypt, treated them cruelly. He forced them to work very hard in the hot, hot sun. He even ordered them to drown their baby boys. One Israelite boy, Moses, was saved by Pharaoh's daughter. When Moses grew up, he told Pharaoh, "Let my people go!" But Pharaoh would not listen.

memories

They ran out of Egypt.

Moses pleaded over and over again with Pharaoh to free the slaves and let them leave Egypt. He warned Pharaoh that God would punish him, but Pharaoh kept saying no.

According to the Bible, God sent ten plagues to Egypt. The last one was so horrible that Pharaoh finally told the Israelites, "Go, but hurry." The Israelites packed quickly. They ran out of Egypt across the desert. At last they were free. The story of how the Israelites escaped to freedom is called the Exodus.

> *The sun rises over the desert in Egypt's Valley of the Kings, where some Pharaohs are buried.*

^ At their school, Israeli children help make matzah for Passover.

Feather

When the Israelites rushed out of Egypt, they had no time to let their bread dough rise before baking it. Instead, it baked right away in the hot desert sun. It became the flat crackers we call matzah. That's why during the week of Passover we cannot eat any *hametz*—foods that need to rise, such as yeast breads and other baked goods.

We search for crumbs.

So before Passover we empty our cupboards of bread, cereal, crackers, cookies, pasta, and pretzels. Before Passover starts, we search for crumbs of hametz left in one room of the house. We use a candle to find the crumbs, and a feather to brush up the crumbs into a wooden spoon.

∨ Rabbi Simcha Levenberg and his family search for hametz in Amherst, Massachusetts. Their kitchen cabinets are covered with foil to make sure no hametz gets into the food they cook for Passover.

By 10 o'clock on the morning of the seder, we have eaten our last hametz for the week. Some of us burn a little bit of bread to symbolically get rid of all the hametz. We think of hametz in another way, too—as our own puffed-up thoughts. We want to get rid of pride.

∧ In Efrat, Israel, a family burns hametz on the morning before the first night of Passover.

> Girls in Toronto, Canada, pack Passover food for people who cannot afford to buy all they need to have a seder.

We think of those who are hungry.

As we watch the flames, we think of those who are hungry and those who suffer. Passover is a time when we give food and money to poor people, too.

∧ Aaron Kintu Moses and his daughter Simcha conduct a hametz-burning ceremony near Mbale, Uganda.

9

∧ Chicken soup with matzah balls

∨ A boy in Connecticut helps his aunt make matzah balls, using an old family recipe.

We cook lots and lots of

food for the seder. We use special pots and pans saved just for Passover. We chop, we boil, we stew, we bake. We use old family recipes to make chicken soup with matzah balls, brisket, turkey with matzah stuffing, roast lamb, gefilte fish, caper-sauce fish, eggplant stew, leek soup, stewed prunes, sweet carrot tzimmes, and haroset. We bake special Passover kugels, matzah pies, macaroons, cakes, and candy.

^ In Morocco, Yamna
*Elfassie cuts onions to
use in her Passover meal.*

We use old family recipes.

We set a beautiful table

for the seder. Some of us use dishes that are used only on Passover. We polish old silver candlesticks and wine goblets called *Kiddush* cups. (Kiddush is the prayer said over wine.) We think of our grandparents and great-grandparents who passed them down to us.

∧ *Seder plate made in Vienna, Austria, 100 years ago*

We set a beautiful table.

We put the special seder plate at the center of the table. On it we place the symbols of Passover, including maror, the bitter herb that reminds us of the bitterness of slavery. We also set aside three special pieces of matzah.

∧ *Engraved silver Kiddush cup*

Elisabeth Rosenfeld prepares the seder plate for her family's Passover meal in Columbus, Ohio.

Everyone has a part.

At last it is time for the seder to begin! Passover, like all Jewish holidays, begins at sundown. Aunts, uncles, cousins, grandparents, and friends come from all over to sit around the table together.

We use a special book called the Haggadah for the seder service. It is filled with prayers, stories, memories, and songs. Everyone has a part in the service. One of the most important parts goes to the youngest child.

< *The Gurwitz family celebrates their seder in San Antonio, Texas.*

∧ *An illustrated Haggadah*

Near the beginning of the seder, the youngest child sings "The Four Questions." The chant begins: *Manishtanah ha lilah ha zeh me kol halaylot?* Why is this night different from all other nights?

Why is this

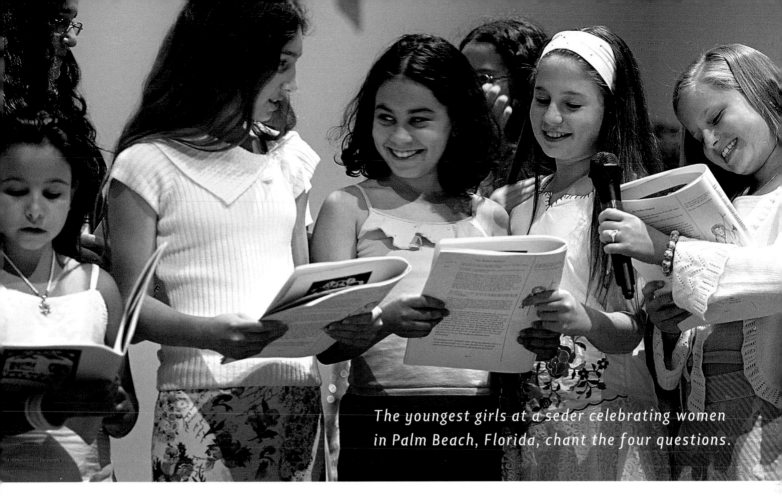

The youngest girls at a seder celebrating women in Palm Beach, Florida, chant the four questions.

night different?

< *Children in Jerusalem, Israel, act out the story of the Exodus at a Passover seder.*

This night is different for many reasons: We have special prayers and rituals at the table before we eat. We sing songs, put on plays, and tell family stories. We eat reclining on pillows to show that we are free and don't have to eat in a rush. Grown-ups drink wine. But we are also serious. We remember when we were slaves in Egypt.

Locust

At the seder we recite the plagues the Bible says God sent to Egypt to punish Pharaoh: BLOOD, FROGS… LOCUSTS…. The last plague was the worst: the death of all firstborn males. God told the Israelites to sacrifice a lamb and smear the lamb's blood over the doorway of their homes. That way the Angel of Death would know to "pass over" their homes. This is where we think Passover got its name.

We recite the plagues.

Frog

As we recite each plague, we take a drop out of our cup of wine or juice with our pinky fingers, because we shouldn't enjoy a full cup while others suffer.

> *Chaya Mushka dips her finger into the wine as her father, Rabbi Shlomo Koves, recites the plagues. Rabbi Koves leads the Chabad Model Seder in Budapest, Hungary, to help young Jews learn how to have a seder.*

We have to find the afikomen.

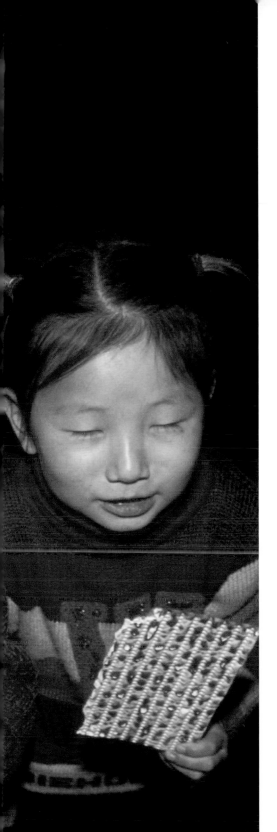

After a lot of prayers and songs, we finally get to eat all that delicious food! But before we can finish the service and go to sleep, we have to find the *afikomen.* This is a piece of the middle matzah that the seder leader hid when we weren't looking. Whoever finds the afikomen gets a present from the leader—a trade so everyone can eat a piece of it and the seder can be finished.

> ∨ *The seder leader gives a prize to the boy who found the afikomen at their seder in Los Angeles, California.*

At a seder in Kaifeng, China, children enjoy a bite of matzah.

Near the end of the service, we open the door for Elijah, the prophet. There is a cup of wine waiting for him. We hear in the Haggadah that one day, Elijah will really come, and he will bring peace on earth.

∨ *A family celebrates freedom and the end of Passover at a park in West Jerusalem, Israel.*

We have

fun together.

∧ Girls enjoy an amusement-park ride in Coney Island, New York, during Passover.

Some families have a seder the next night, too. Passover lasts about a week. During that week, we can't eat bread, cereal, pretzels, or any other kind of hametz. But we eat lots of matzah, and we have fun together.

We celebrate
our freedom.

*A father takes a picture of his children
playing on the beach at Coney Island,
New York, during Passover.*

During Passover we celebrate our freedom. It is important to remember that we were once slaves in Egypt. There is nothing better than being free!

MORE ABOUT PASSOVER

Contents

Just the Facts

WHO CELEBRATES IT: Jews

WHAT IT IS: A holiday to celebrate the Israelites' freedom from slavery in Egypt. It was the beginning of the Exodus in the desert.

WHEN IT STARTS: It begins at sundown on the evening before the 15th day of the Hebrew month of Nissan, which is usually in April.

HOW LONG: Jews in Israel and Reform Jews observe Passover for seven days. Most Conservative, Orthodox, and Reconstructionist Jews observe it for eight days.

RITUAL: The seder, a long meal with prayers, stories, and special foods, with the Haggadah as the guide. People recline on pillows because the slaves had to eat in a hurry but free people could eat in a leisurely manner.

ALSO KNOWN AS: Pesach, the Hebrew word that means "he passed over" or possibly "guarding." Some people refer to it also as the Festival of Freedom, the Festival of Unleavened Bread, or the Festival of Spring.

FOOD: Unleavened bread called matzah, and food made with it. Eating leavened foods is forbidden.

The Four Questions

This part of the seder is to hold the attention of the children and to begin the story of the Israelites in Egypt. That's why the youngest child has the important job of asking the four questions. Sometimes two or more children share. One might say them in English, the other in Hebrew. Below are the four questions in English. You will see that there are really five if you count the first one!

WHY IS THIS NIGHT DIFFERENT FROM ALL OTHER NIGHTS?

1

On all other nights we eat leavened bread or matzah; why on this night only matzah?

2

On all other nights we eat all kinds of herbs; why on this night do we eat especially bitter herbs?

3

On all other nights we do not dip herbs at all; why on this night do we dip them twice?

4

On all other nights we eat either sitting or reclining; why on this night do we eat in a reclining position?

The Symbols of the Seder Plate

The seder plate is the center of the seder table. We put on it the symbols of Passover. Different families might place additional foods on the seder plate, but these are the basic symbolic items we use:

∨ *Decorations on the empty seder plate show the symbols of Passover. These foods fill the bottom plate.*

Maror (mah-ROAR): the bitter herb (usually horseradish) that reminds us of the hard times the Israelites had when they were slaves in Egypt.

Hazeret (hah-ZAIR-et): a second bitter herb; often one such as romaine lettuce, which tastes sweet at first and then bitter, because at first the Israelites had a good life in Egypt.

Haroset (ha-ROW-set): a mixture of fruit, nuts, and wine that looks like the bricks and mortar the slaves used—but tastes delicious. Also spelled *haroseth*.

Z'roah (Ze-ROW ah): a roasted shank bone, because in the old days the Israelites sacrificed a lamb at Passover. The night before they left Egypt, the Israelites sacrificed a lamb and put the lamb's blood above their doors. Then the Angel of Death knew to pass over their homes and not kill their firstborn sons (the last plague).

Karpas (car-PAHS): a green vegetable, usually a sprig of parsley, which stands for spring and new life. We dip the karpas in salt water to mix new life with tears. The salted water also reminds us of the Red Sea, which God parted to let the Israelites escape.

Beitzah: (bay-TZAH): a roasted egg, another symbol of the ancient sacrifice, and also a symbol of life.

Passover Toffee

There are many great Passover recipes. My sons love this one. It is so delicious! It's easy to make, but you will need an adult to help you.

INGREDIENTS:
matzah (about 4 sheets)
1 cup (2 sticks) unsalted butter
1 cup firmly packed brown sugar
1 cup chocolate chips
1/2 cup chopped nuts (optional)

YOU WILL ALSO NEED:
A cookie sheet
Aluminum foil

1. Cover the cookie sheet with aluminum foil, shiny side up.

2. Cover the foil with a layer of matzah. You can break the matzah up to fit, but try to keep the pieces large.

3. Preheat the oven to 325°F.

4. Heat the butter and the brown sugar together in a saucepan over medium heat. Stir constantly with a wooden spoon, mixing the sugar with the butter as it melts. Once the mixture is smooth and thick, spoon it over the matzah, spreading it to the edges.

5. Put the cookie sheet in the oven and bake the matzah for about 8 to 10 minutes, or until it starts to bubble. Watch it so it doesn't burn.

6. Remove the matzah from the oven, sprinkle it with chocolate chips, then put the matzah back in the oven. Take it out once the chocolate chips just start to melt.

7. Spread the chocolate evenly with a spatula.

8. Sprinkle half the toffee with nuts, if you'd like.

9. Leave the toffee on the cookie sheet and cool it on a rack. Then put it in the freezer for at least one hour. Once the toffee is frozen, break it into pieces and enjoy. Yum!

The Ten Plagues

Fly

Listed by their Hebrew names, these are the ten plagues that God sent to Egypt, in the order in which they occurred.

Dam (blood): The water in all the rivers, lakes, etc. in Egypt turned to blood.

Tsfardeia (frogs): Millions of frogs fell all over the land.

Kinim (lice): All the Egyptians and their animals got lice.

Arov (flies or wild animals): Whichever they were, there were too many of them!

Dever (cattle disease): All livestock got sick.

Shkhin (boils): All the Egyptians (and their livestock) got nasty sores that wouldn't heal.

Barad (hail mixed with fire): A storm like that you wouldn't want to live through.

Arbeh (locusts): There were locusts everywhere. They killed all the plants and trees.

Hosheh (darkness): For three days there was utter darkness.

Makat Bechorot (death of the firstborn): The Angel of Death killed all the firstborn sons in Egypt; every Egyptian home suffered a loss.

Find Out More

BOOKS

The books with a star (*) are especially good for children.

*Golden, Barbara Diamond. *The Passover Journey*. Viking, 1994. Good information about the history of Passover and the seder.

*Herman, Debbie, and Ann D. Koffsky. *More Than Matzah*. Barron's, 2006. Crafts, recipes, and activities for the seder.

*Kimmel, Eric A. *Wonders and Miracles*. Scholastic Press, 2004. A wonderful book to read as a family before and during Passover.

*Musleah, Rahel. *Why on This Night?* Simon & Schuster, 2000. A lovely Haggadah for parents and children to share.

Pleck, Elizabeth H. *Celebrating the Family: Ethnicity, Consumer Culture, and Family Rituals*. Harvard University Press, 2000. Chapter 5 looks at the history and sociology of Passover.

*Zalben, Jane Breskin. *Pearl's Passover*. Simon & Schuster, 2002. Fiction and fun activities.

WEB SITES

www.myjewishlearning.com/ article/passover-pesach
Seder customs around the world.

www.miriamscup.com
This site tells about Miriam's Cup, a new ritual to honor Miriam, the sister of Moses.

www.ritualwell.org/parts-seder
This site explains the significance of the parts of the seder.

EDUCATIONAL EXTENSIONS

Reading

1. How does the story of Moses and the Exodus explain why Jews eat matzah at Passover?

2. What are some of the rituals involved in the seder and what do they symbolize for Jews?

3. Pick a favorite photograph from the text and reread its caption. What symbols of Passover can you see in the details of the image? (Hint: Expand upon the information given and the details observed visually in relation to the context of the page.)

Writing

4. Write an informative/explanatory essay about the use of special seder plates during Passover. Explain their role in the seder meal and the symbolism behind the contents.

Speaking & Listening

5. Present your explanatory essay to your class, friends, or parents. Make your own seder plate to use as a visual display of the information you are presenting.

Glossary

Afikomen (ah-fee-KOH-men): A piece of the middle matzah hidden by the leader of the seder, found by the children, and then eaten by all for dessert.

Elijah (Ee-LIE-jah): A prophet from the Bible. Some Jews believe he will return to foretell the coming of the Messiah, or savior.

Haggadah (Hah-god-DAH): The book used to conduct the seder service. Haggadah means telling.

Hametz (Ha-METZ): Foods that need to rise.

Maror (mah-ROAR): A bitter herb.

Matzah (mah-TZAH): Bread that has not risen.

Plague: A widespread calamity.

Prophet: A person who people believe speaks for God.

Seder (SEH-der): The ritual service held at Passover.

Tzimmes (TZIH-miss): A sweet stew usually made with carrots and prunes.

Where This Book's Photos Were Taken

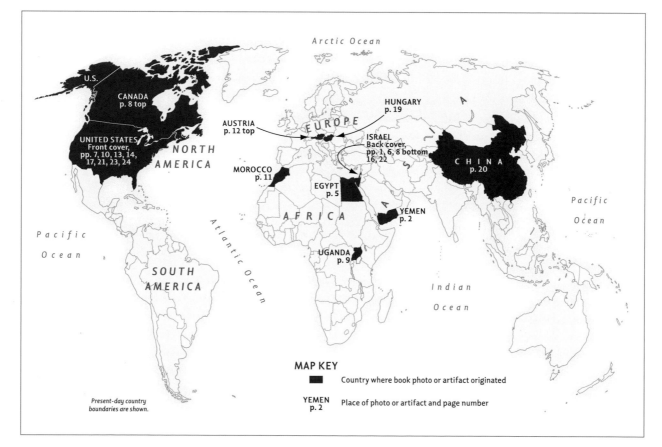

Arctic Ocean

U.S.

CANADA
p. 8 top

EUROPE

HUNGARY
p. 19

AUSTRIA
p. 12 top

ISRAEL
Back cover,
pp. 1, 6, 8 bottom,
16, 22

NORTH
AMERICA

UNITED STATES
Front cover,
pp. 7, 10, 13, 14,
17, 21, 23, 24

CHINA
p. 20

MOROCCO
p. 11

EGYPT
p. 5

Pacific
Ocean

Pacific
Ocean

Atlantic Ocean

AFRICA

YEMEN
p. 2

SOUTH
AMERICA

UGANDA
p. 9

Indian
Ocean

MAP KEY

Country where book photo or artifact originated

YEMEN
p. 2   Place of photo or artifact and page number

Present-day country boundaries are shown.

Passover: A Celebration of Freedom

by Rabbi Shira Stern

Why is this holiday different from all other holidays? On every Jewish holiday we remember the story associated with the holiday. On Passover, however, we use our five senses to recreate the experience of the Israelites' passage from slavery to freedom, so that the words "when we were freed from Egypt" become real to us.

We do this at the ritual service of prayers, stories, and special foods known as the seder, which means "order," as in order of events. The seder usually has 15 parts as set forth in the *Hagaddah*. Hagaddah means "telling," and the seder is the telling of the Exodus story (Exodus 1:8-15:21). It is important for each generation to pass down the story to the next. Many families pass down special traditions as well, both serious and funny. Sections such as the four questions and the hiding of the *afikomen* are designed to keep the children entertained. The afikomen is the middle of three pieces of matzah. Why do we have three pieces of matzah? At each Jewish holiday we are supposed to have two whole loaves of bread. On Passover we add a third, broken one—the bread of affliction.

Although there are different ways to have a seder, almost everyone includes the same main elements. You will notice a preponderance of fours—four questions, four sons, four cups of wine. That is because in Exodus, God promises four times to redeem the Israelites.

The four questions: The youngest child able asks these questions, in a Hebrew chant if possible. These questions help shape the framework of the seder. The idea is that the seder will answer them.

The four sons: Four sons ask about the seder—the wise son, the angry son, the simple-minded son, and the son who cannot ask. This is to ensure that everyone, even those who don't know enough to ask, get to hear the historical tale.

Four cups of wine: During the seder adults are supposed to drink four full cups of wine. Many Jews add a fifth cup of wine at the seder to remember the oppression that still exists in the world, and we pray that the oppressed will soon be free. Some Jews add a new cup, one filled with water, to honor Miriam, Moses' older sister, who helped save him when he was a baby by putting him in a basket in the river for Pharaoh's daughter to find. It is said that wherever Miriam went, a well of pure water was found.

Reciting the plagues: As we recite the plagues we take a drop of wine out of our cup with our pinkies because in a *midrash,* a rabbinic story, the angels are seen celebrating the safe passage of the Israelites but God, crying, mourns also for the Egyptians who died following Pharaoh's orders. We do not celebrate at the expense of those innocents who are suffering.

Thinking of others and social change are themes that are made current by new additions to the seder. Some families include an orange on the seder plate, which clearly does not belong there, representing all who feel left out of society.

Seders in different parts of the world share a great many things, but they also differ. For example, Jews from Eastern Europe (Ashkenazim) do not eat rice nor include lamb in the holiday meal, while Jews from Arabic and African countries (Sephardim) *include* rice and serve lamb to remember the first night of the Exodus. During Passover we are not allowed the five main grains: wheat, barley, oats, rye, and spelt, and all liquids containing grain alcohol. Bread, leavened cakes, cookies, biscuits, crackers, cereals, beer, and whiskey are not permitted for those observing the laws of Passover. Canned and boxed items need to have a "kosher for Passover" label to be considered kosher. If it gets confusing—and it is for many of us—ask a rabbi.

The message of Passover and the seder is a universal and ageless one: Freedom makes everything—not just a single night—different.

Rabbi Shira Stern is a pastoral counselor and chaplain in Marlboro, N.J., and director of the Center for Pastoral Care and Counseling.

For my family, especially all the Elijahs.

PICTURE CREDITS

Front cover: Lori Epstein/National Geographic Creative; Back cover: © Ronen Zvulun/Corbis; Spine: © Ewa Walicka/Shutterstock; Pages 1, 8 top: © Yehoshua Halevi/Golden Light Images; Page 2: © H. Armstrong Roberts/Robertstock.com; Page 3: © Ewa Walicka/Shutterstock; Pages 4-5: © Kenneth Garrett/National Geographic/Getty Images; Page 6 top: © Ronen Zvulun/Reuters; Page 6 bottom: © Olga Shelego/Shutterstock; Page 7: © Mario Tama/Getty Images; Page 8 bottom: © Stephen Epstein/PonkaWonka.com; Page 9: © Chaya Weinstein/PonkaWonka.com; Page 10 top: © OdeliaCohen/Digital Stock; Page 10 bottom: © Christopher Fitzgerald/The Image Works; Page 11: © Bryan Schwartz; Page 12 top: © The Jewish Museum/Art Resource, NY; Pages 12 bottom, 16 top: © Andy Crawford/Dorling Kindersley; Page 13: © Ira Block; Pages 14-15: © William Luther/San Antonio Express-News/ZUMA Press; Page 16 bottom: © Richard T. Nowitz/Corbis; Page 17: © Thomas Cordy/Palm Beach Post/ZUMA Press; Page 18 top: © Alan Smillie/Shutterstock; Page 18 bottom: © Joanne Harris & Daniel Bubnich/Shutterstock; Page 19: © Zsolt Demecs/Chabad.org; Pages 20-21: © Dvir Bar-Gal/ZUMA Press; Page 21 right: © Michael Newman/Photo Edit; Page 22: © Annie Griffiths Belt/Corbis; Page 23: © Mary Altaffer/Associated Press; Pages 24-25: © Les Stone/ZUMA Press; Pages 27 top, 27 bottom: © Dorling Kindersley/Getty Images; Page 28: © Marfé Ferguson Delano; Page 29: © Dhoxax/Shutterstock.

Text copyright © 2007 Deborah Heiligman
Reprinted in paperback and library binding, 2017

The Library of Congress cataloged the 2007 edition as follows:

Library of Congress Cataloging-in-Publication Data
Heiligman, Deborah.
Holidays around the world : celebrate Passover with matzah, maror, and memories / Deborah Heiligman ; consultant, Shira Stern.
    p. cm. — (Holidays around the world)
ISBN-13: 978-1-4263-0018-9 (hardcover)
ISBN-13: 978-1-4263-0019-6 (library binding)
1. Passover — Juvenile literature. I. Title.
    BM695.P3H374 2006
    296.4'37 — dc22
                        2006020676

2017 paperback edition ISBN: 978-1-4263-2745-2
2017 reinforced library binding edition ISBN: 978-1-4263-2746-9

National Geographic supports K–12 educators with ELA Common Core Resources. Visit natgeoed.org/commoncore for more information.

Series design by 3+Co. and Jim Hiscott.
The body text in the book is set in Mrs. Eaves.
The display text is Lisboa.

Front cover: A girl presents a seder plate, which holds the symbols of Passover.
Back cover: Israeli children in Gaza make homemade matzah.
Title page: Liora Halevi searches for the last bits of hametz with her family in their home in Israel.

Printed in Hong Kong
16/THK/1

Since 1888, the National Geographic Society has funded more than 12,000 research, exploration, and preservation projects around the world. The Society receives funds from National Geographic Partners, LLC, funded in part by your purchase. A portion of the proceeds from this book supports this vital work. To learn more, visit natgeo.com/info.

NATIONAL GEOGRAPHIC and Yellow Border Design are trademarks of the National Geographic Society, used under license.

For more information, visit nationalgeographic.com, call 1-800-647-5463, or write to the following address:
National Geographic Partners
1145 17th Street N.W.
Washington, D.C. 20036-4688 U.S.A.

For information about special discounts for bulk purchases, please contact National Geographic Books Special Sales: specialsales@natgeo.com

For rights or permissions inquiries, please contact National Geographic Books Subsidiary Rights: bookrights@natgeo.com

STAFF FOR THIS BOOK

Nancy Laties Feresten, *Vice President, Editor-in-Chief of Children's Books*
Bea Jackson, *Design and Illustrations Director, Children's Books*
Sanjida Rashid, *Associate Designer*
Amy Shields, *Executive Editor, Children's Books*
Marfé Ferguson Delano, *Project Editor*
Lori Epstein, *Illustrations Editor*
Melissa Brown, *Project Designer*
Sanjida Rashid and Rachel Kenny, *Design Production Assistants*
Carl Mehler, *Director of Maps*
Priyanka Lamichhane, *Assistant Editor*
Rebecca Baines, *Editorial Assistant*
Paige Towler, *Editorial Assistant*
R. Gary Colbert, *Production Director*
Lewis R. Bassford, *Production Manager*
Vincent P. Ryan, Maryclare Tracy, *Manufacturing Managers*
Kelsey Carlson, *Education Consultant*

ACKNOWLEDGMENTS

Thanks to: Rabbi Shira Stern who is a great help and always right there; Rabbi Don Weber, who can drive and teach at the same time; Rabbi Sandy Roth, who lent me books and always lends me wisdom; Vivian Philips who gave me the toffee recipe years ago; and to my friends who told me what their families eat at Seder, especially Mary Wiener (caper-sauce fish?). Thanks to Marfé Delano for keeping me sane and to Lori Epstein for sending me photos that make me laugh (in addition to finding the beautiful ones in this book). A special thanks to my wonderful family: my sister Linnie, who makes seder every year; her husband, Mike, who leads it (though now that there are so many little kids, Mike, I think it has to be shorter); to Phil, who made us laugh until he got too tired; to Essie, who puts up with Phil; and to all the new Elijahs who have picked up the job: Aaron (Elijahbunny), Benjamin (sorry about the Michael Jordan game), Tinka (a dog in a kipa!), and all the future Elijahs: Elizabeth, Natalie, Caroline, Julia, Matthew, Andrew, Katie, Henry, and Owen. And Jon, thanks for putting up with it all.